Voices From Canada's Past

Book One
Historical Biographies

Voices From Canada's Past

Book One
Historical Biographies

Editor: Gladys E. Neale

EACH ONE TEACH ONE

LAUBACH LITERACY OF CANADA

Copyright © 1990 by Laubach Literacy of Canada
ISBN 0-920877-22-2

Canadian Cataloguing in Publication Data

Main entry under title:

Voices from Canada's past : historical biographies
    book 1

ISBN 0-920877-22-2

1. Readers for new literates.   2. Canada — Biography.
I. Neale, Gladys E.   II. Laubach Literacy of
Canada.

PE1126.N43V6 1990   428.6'2   C90-093367-4

Every effort has been made to locate and acknowledge the correct
copyright owners.

Typeset by Video Text Inc., Barrie, Ontario

Printed and bound in Canada by D.W. Friesen, Altona, Manitoba

Published by
Laubach Literacy of Canada
P.O. Box 6548
Station "A",
Saint John, New Brunswick
E2L 4R9

Contents

Acknowledgments

Our grateful appreciation to the Canadian Give the Gift of Literacy Foundation whose grant of $3000 assisted us in the publishing of this book.

We wish to express our thanks to the National Archives of Canada, Metropolitan Toronto Library Board, the Provincial Archives of British Columbia and the Provincial Archives of Manitoba for the photographs used in this book. Their staffs were most helpful in locating suitable photographs for us. The pages on which their photographs appear are noted below.

Illustrations:

Key to abbreviations

NAC	National Archives of Canada
MTLB	Metropolitan Toronto Library Board
PABC	Provincial Archives of British Columbia
PA Man	Provincial Archives of Manitoba

p. 2 NAC/C16753; p. 10 NAC/C5136; p. 12 MTLB; p. 14 MTLB; p. 18 NAC/23384; p. 20 MTLB; p. 21 NAC/C119889; p. 23 NAC/C40241; p. 24 NAC/C5560; p. 27 NAC/C10687; p. 29 NAC/C10690; p. 30 NAC/C12329; p. 35 NAC/C3202; p. 37 MTLB; p. 38 NAC/C11222; p. 41; MTLB; p. 45 MTLB; p. 46 NAC/C6296; p. 49 NAC/C788; p. 51 MTLB; p. 53 NAC/PA45863; p. 54 NAC/C938; p. 58 NAC/C10717; p. 59 MTLB; p. 61 MTLB; p. 64 NAC/C124; p. 67 MTLB; p. 68 PABC/WP39858; p. 70 PA Man/N10100; p. 72 PABC/85186; p. 74 PABC/HP39854; p. 75 PABC/HP39849; p. 76 PABC/HP75437; p. 77 PABC/HP39853; p. 78 NAC/C8015; p. 83 NAC/PA141882; p. 85 NAC/PA172655; p. 86 NAC/PA155156.

Introduction

This book of Canadian historical biographies has two purposes: (1) to give those who have just learned to read, interesting stories at an easy reading level and (2) to give a background of Canadian history through biographies.

Once students have reading skills, to keep and improve them, they need more and more reading materials. This book was developed to meet this important need.

Our hope is that readers will enjoy these biographies and will also appreciate those men and women whose efforts built firm foundations for our country.

Laubach Literacy of Canada

Leif Ericson, Norseman

by
Michael Collins

This monument of Lief Ericson is in Boston, U.S.A.

THE CALL TO ADVENTURE

Leif Ericson's friend, Harald, came across the rocky pasture field. "Bjarni Herjolfsson is back from Norway!" he cried. "His ship is in the fjord. He's coming to Brattalid to trade the last of his goods. This is his last trading journey. He is going to work on his father's farm."

Leif was surprised that Bjarni was planning to stop sailing.

"If we can get his ship," Harald was excited. "We can sail to the new lands he saw a few years ago. He saw them when he lost his way in a storm."

"He will want much in barter for his ship." Leif said.

The two young men were about twenty years old. They were skilled in farming and sailing the rough seas around Greenland.

"Let's talk with your father." Harald was on his way to the Ericson's stone and wooden farm buildings.

"No," Leif laughed. "Father is asleep after the mid-day meal. He's not as young as when he led the expedition of settlers here. Wait until Bjarni comes. We should talk to him first."

A crowd met Bjarni's ship when it put into Brattalid. The town was near the Ericson farm. When the bartering was finished for the goods, Leif and Harald talked with Bjarni. Their talk was of the new lands he had seen. They wanted to know the best way to sail there.

THE PLANS

"Sail with Greenland to your right hand for two suns," he told them. "Turn away from Greenland for two more suns. Ahead you will see a land of glaciers. Then sail to the setting sun for days. Now you will see a land covered with trees. The sea current will help your ship along."

They listened to Bjarni. Leif invited him to dinner at the Ericson farm. He could meet Leif's father, Eric the Red.

They talked late into the night. The Ericsons bartered cows and other animals for Bjarni's ship. Eric the Red agreed to lead the search for these new lands.

The next day Bjarni loaded the cows and other animals on the ship. Then he sailed to where his father farmed. Harald had found a small crew of men. With them Leif went with Bjarni. They brought the ship back to Brattalid.

While they were away, Harald found men for the rest of the crew. They got all their supplies ready for the voyage. The supplies were safe in leather sacks.

A Viking Ship.

THE VOYAGE BEGINS

Days later the ship was loaded and ready to leave. But Eric the Red could not lead them. He had hurt himself a few days earlier when riding his horse. Now Leif was the leader.

The next morning the crew rowed the ship down the fjord. They raised the square-cut sail. It filled in the light wind. Leif, at the steering oar, pointed the ship into the open sea.

They sailed and rowed this way for two suns. They then turned so that the afternoon sun was on their left hand. They sailed another two days. On the second day, they saw a land covered with glaciers. They brought the ship into sheltered waters.

HELLULAND

Leif, Harald and two crewmen went ashore in their small boat. The land was covered with flat stones, from the shore to the glaciers.

"A sheep would starve here," Harald said.

Leif kicked at one of the flat stones with his seal-skin boot. "Because the land is covered with these stones, we could call this place Helluland."

The others thought it was a good name. Then they went back to the ship and sailed on.

MARKLAND

They sailed towards the setting sun. Days passed and they saw a land covered with trees. They passed a long, wide, sandy beach. They went ashore near the end of the beach.

"We need wood in Greenland," Harald said, eyeing the trees along the shore. "This is where we can get that wood."

Leif smiled at that. "Because this is a wooded land, we will name this place Markland."

They filled their empty water-skins. They went back to the ship and set sail again. They lost sight of land. On the second day of sailing from the wide sandy beach, they saw a narrow neck of land pushing seawards. They sailed in between this land and some islands. They sailed into a small bay.

THE FIRST SETTLEMENT

This land was different. Trees were plentiful. There was also grass-covered land, from the shore to the trees.

"This is better," Leif said to Harald. "We can feed animals here and farm."

"It could be a good place for a settlement," Harald agreed. "There is a lot of grass growing here. You should call it Vinland, after the meadows in Greenland."

"Vinland it shall be." Leif said. Then he told him, "Get the crew to move the ship in closer to shore. At high tide we will bring the ship into that small brook we see from here."

6

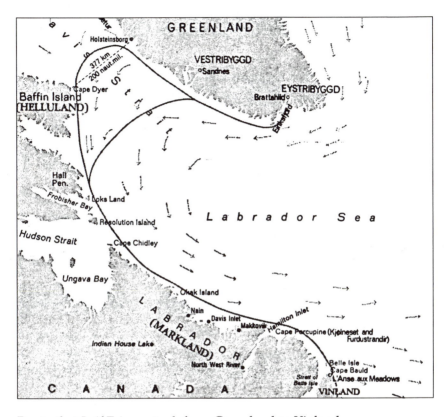

Route that Leif Ericson took from Greenland to Vinland.

Leif and his men built two large sod-covered houses. They stayed there until the next summer. Then they loaded their ship with wood and other things that grew in this new land. They returned to Brattalid in Greenland.

They were the first men from the old World to land and live in North America. This was in the year 1000 A.D.

A sod-covered house.

AFTER THE ADVENTURE

Leif Ericson did not return to Vinland. Other Norsemen tried to settle this new land. Leif's houses were used by these Vikings as their base. Their efforts at settlement lasted only a few years. The sod houses that Leif and his men had built sank back into the earth.

In 1961, in Northern Newfoundland, a Viking site was found. The site was near a place called L'Anse aux Meadows, the Cove of Meadows. There was the outline of Norse houses in the meadow. Viking articles of a thousand years ago were also discovered at L'Anse aux Meadows. This is the only known Viking site in North America. L'Anse aux Meadows is believed to be the place where Leif and his crew lived long ago.

Little more is known about Leif Ericson. His son was made Chief at Brattalid, in the year 1025 A.D. Leif may have died shortly before this event.

After that date, the name Ericson disappeared from Greenland history. Only in the old Norse stories do we learn about the deeds of discovery by the young man named Leif Ericson.

John Cabot

by
Michael Collins

IMAGINARY MEDALLION PORTRAIT
OF JOHN CABOT.
By Carlo Barrera Pezzi. From
a memoir published in Venice in 1881.

CABOT'S EARLY YEARS

John Cabot was born in 1449 in Genoa, a city in Italy. When he was a young man he went to live in Venice, another city in Italy. He became an expert sailor and he learned how to make maps. He became a merchant in the spice trade. He brought spices into Europe from the Near East.

Cabot was also interested in Cathay, which was then the name for China. Spices came from the spice islands of Cathay. This faraway land filled John Cabot's mind with ideas.

He thought that the world was round. If so, and he sailed west instead of east, he would reach Cathay. The merchants of Venice were interested in Cabot's ideas about sailing westward. They were not interested enough to provide him with money for a ship and a crew. As well as money, Cabot needed a crew who knew about the winds and sailing on the western seas.

MOVE TO ENGLAND

About 1495, Cabot and his family moved to England, to the port of Bristol. Bristol was a well-known seafaring port. There sailors lived who were skilled in sailing the western seas. The merchants of Bristol were interested in Cabot's ideas about sailing westward to Cathay. In 1496 they helped Cabot get permission from the English King, Henry the Seventh, to sail in search of Cathay. They provided money for a ship and a crew.

FIRST VOYAGE

People believed then that there was an island west of Ireland. It was called the Isle of Brasil.

Cabot made a voyage to find this island. He wanted an island to use as a base for his search for Cathay. Bad weather frightened his crew. Then a shortage of food forced Cabot and his crew back to Bristol. They had not found any island.

This shows the flag given by Henry VII to Cabot.

SECOND VOYAGE

The next year Cabot once more set sail. This was the voyage which would take him to the land he thought was Cathay. He sailed from Bristol on the 2nd of May, 1497 in a small carvel. Carvels were sturdy ships built to sail on the rough, open seas. This carvel was named the "Matthew". It was a small ship. It had a crew of eighteen men.

Cabot and his crew landed somewhere in North America on the 24th of June, 1497. He and his crew went ashore on the wooded land. Cabot took possession of the land in the name of Henry the Seventh.

They saw some simple shelters but no people. Cabot did not explore inland. He and his crew returned to the "Matthew". They sailed along the coast eastward for a month. Then they returned to Bristol.

The Matthew.

A POPULAR MAN

Cabot told King Henry that he had found Cathay. He had taken possession of the land in the King's name. The King granted Cabot a small pension for life.

The Bristol merchants were not interested in this new land. They were interested in a part of Cabot's report to the King. This said that the seas near this land were full of fish. Fish was a popular food in Europe. If there were many fish, then the Bristol merchants could make fortunes. They could do this by catching, salting and drying the fish, and selling it in Europe.

Cabot made a map of his voyage. He became a popular man in Bristol.

King Henry was interested in Cathay, as a possession for England. He listened to Cabot's plans for a new voyage. The King agreed to provide a ship and crew. The Bristol merchants agreed to give Cabot four more ships for this second voyage to Cathay.

LAST VOYAGE

With his five ships and a crew of three hundred men, Cabot sailed from Bristol in May, 1498. He planned to sail to his first landfall. Then he would sail southward where he thought he would reach the spice islands of Cathay. The ships carried food for a voyage of one year.

The five ships sailed around the south of Ireland. A storm damaged Cabot's ship. He had to return to a port in Ireland for repairs. The ships sailed to Greenland. They crossed the seas to Baffinland and sailed down the coast of North America. They followed the same route Leif Ericson and his crew had taken, five hundred years earlier. The ships sailed as far south as what is now known as Chesapeake Bay.

Cabot did not find the spice islands of Cathay. Probably he did not know that he was sailing along the coast of a new land. His food supplies began to run low. He turned his ships towards England and their home port of Bristol.

But John Cabot never reached Bristol. Somewhere off the coast of Newfoundland, his ships must have been caught in a wild storm. One or two of the ships may have returned to Bristol. No written record remains to tell us if this happened. John Cabot disappeared without a trace.

CABOT FOUND NORTH AMERICA

Historians do not agree about the place where John Cabot made his first landing in North America. Cape North, on Cape Breton Island, may be the most likely place. There is a plaque at Cape North which tells us Cabot and his crew landed there on the 24th of June, 1497.

Cabot's discovery of these new lands opened the way for more exploration by Europeans. First, fishermen came to fish in the waters off this new land. These settlers came to clear the land and farm. Cabot thought he had sailed westward and found Cathay. Instead he had found a new world. He had found the land we know as North America.

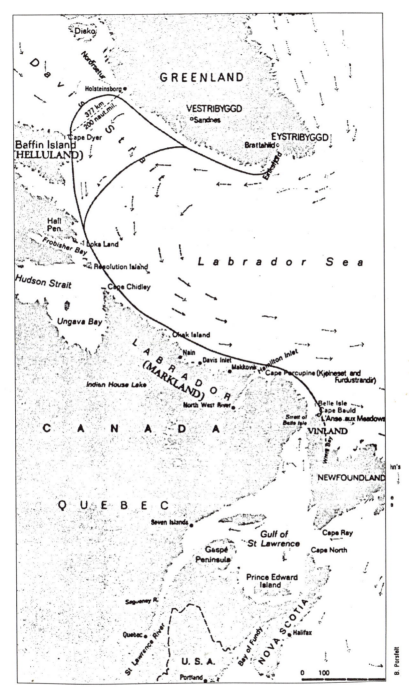

Cabot followed the same route as Ericson.

17

Early Life in New France

by
Bernice Cleator

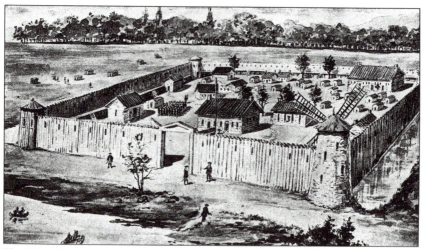

The Verchères Fort.

TROUBLE FOR THE SETTLERS

The years before our story had been very hard. There wasn't much of Canada then. There were just a few settlements along the St. Lawrence River. The Indians had lived there for a very long time. They did not want the white people to settle there. They wanted to get rid of them. Some of the Indian tribes were friendly, but not the Iroquois.

The Iroquois killed every settler they saw. They kept watch on the settlements. They caught anyone who stepped outside. They burned the corn and grain. They did not let the farmers work in the fields.

The settlers had come from France. The settlements were called New France. Now the King of France must do something to help them. He sent a large army of soldiers. They were to get rid of the Iroquois. But how? They came up with a plan. They would march on the Iroquois villages. They would make the Indians fight or give up.

The Indians in the villages would not fight. They would not give up. They just left the villages. They slipped off into the woods. The army would burn the villages and march on. But the soldiers never got any Iroquois with this plan.

They tried other plans. Every plan failed. The Iroquois had the upper hand.

At the end of a tour of duty, the soldiers were very glad to go home to France.

ANOTHER PLAN

Now the King came up with another plan. He would give large grants of land to the best army officers. He would give them money to clear the land. This way he could keep the best men in Canada. They would become seigneurs. The lands they were given would be their seigneuries. The men who had served under the officers would become their tenants.

All of these men were soldiers. They would be settlers and soldiers too. In this way the King got protection for his settlements.

The river was the only way to travel. There were roads. Boats were used in the summer and sleds in the winter. All the seigneuries faced the river.

A Manor House.

SEIGNEURIES

The large house built for the seigneur and his family was called the manor house. Smaller houses were built around the manor house. In these lived the tenants. The tenants were called habitants.

All the time the building was going on, the Iroquois were watching. They were ready to pounce on a worker who got too far away. Some of the habitants had to stand guard while the others worked. They took turns at guard duty. The seigneur worked too. All hands were needed.

Walls sixteen feet high were built around the buildings. To get inside the walls you had to go through one gate. The gate faced the river.

Other buildings were needed inside the walls too. Store-houses and barns and woodsheds were built. A vegetable garden was begun.

The Mill.

The area inside the walls was called the fort.

One of the most important buildings inside the fort was the mill. Here the habitants would bring their grain. The grain would be ground into flour. The mill was also a look-out. The top of it had holes facing all ways. The man on guard in the look-out could shoot through the holes.

Then the men turned to the large area behind the fort. These lands had to be cleared to grow crops. The men working there had to keep their guns close at hand. Many men were killed by the Iroquois who were watching from the woods.

It was the seigneur's job to keep order in his seigneury. He also tried to keep his people happy. Each year he had them all in to the manor house for a big party.

A BAD YEAR

Life could have gone well in the settlements of New France. Nothing could stop the Iroquois.

1690 was a very bad year. The Iroquois wanted to put an end to the settlements. They hid along the river banks. They killed anyone who set foot in a canoe. No one could go anywhere. They watched the fields at the back of the seigneuries. No one could work on the farm lands. The seigneuries were in bad shape. The buildings and walls needed repairs. No one could go out to work on them. The people had little to eat.

At last 500 men were sent from Montreal. They were to stand guard over all the settlements. The seigneurs and the habitants could now get back on the land. Men, women and children turned out to work in the fields. That was a busy summer. For a while the raids stopped.

Over the roofs of Verchères.

Girl of New France

by
Bernice Cleator

An artist's impression of Madeleine de Verchères.

"THE IROQUOIS ARE HERE"

It was early morning, October, 1692.

Madeleine de Verchères passed through the gate of the fort. She walked down to the bank of the river. She was looking at her father's boats.

Suddenly a shot rang out. Shouts of pain came from the fields behind the fort. A woman cried out, "Run, Mademoiselle, run, the Iroquois are here."

Madeleine had heard shouts like that before. The Iroquois Indians were killing the men in the fields. They were coming to attack the fort.

She turned to run. If she could only get to the gate! About 45 Iroquois began to run around the fort from the fields. They were running toward her. They began to fire shots at her. The shots rang all around her head as she ran.

Just a few more steps to go. But one Indian was faster than the others. He caught the cape she had over her shoulders. She thought she was finished. She got free of the cape. She took hold of the gate and slammed it in his face.

Madeleine was inside the fort. Now what should she do?

THE VERCHERES FAMILY

At the time of our story Madeleine was only fourteen years old. She lived with her family in the fort on their seigneury. The Verchères seigneury was on the St. Lawrence River. It was between Montreal and Quebec. All the seigneuries faced the river. The long narrow fields stretched out behind the fort.

Madeleine was the daughter of the seigneur of Verchères.

The seigneur and his wife had twelve children. Madeleine's older sister was married. Her young husband had been killed by the Iroquois. Madeleine's older brother was killed at the age of sixteen. He was helping a neighbour when his seigneury was attacked by 300 Indians.

Madeleine grew up with the Indian wars all around her. Her father, the seigneur of Verchères, was a brave army officer. He taught his children to be brave too.

On that morning in October, 1692, the seigneur was not at home. He had been called to Quebec to report for duty as an army officer. Madeleine's mother was in Montreal.

"WE MUST FIGHT"

In the fort were Madeleine, her two younger brothers, an old man of eighty, two soldiers, a servant and a few women and small children. The men were at work in the fields.

When Madeleine ran into the fort and slammed the gate against the Indian, there was little help. The two soldiers were hiding in a corner, stiff with fear. The women and children were crying. It was their men who were being killed in the farm fields.

Madeleine took command. She grabbed a soldier's helmet that was hanging on the wall. She put it on her long fair hair. She picked up a gun. She found guns for her little brothers. She shouted to the two soldiers.

"We must fight to the death", she cried. She knew what her father would have done. Now she made up her mind to take his place.

Madeleine slams the gate.

She knew that parts of the walls needed repairs. They were weak. She placed the soldiers and her two little brothers at the weak places in the walls. They kept firing out at the Iroquois. She saw something that made her heart sink.

HELP COMES

A seigneur from nearby was paddling home from Montreal. He had his family in the big canoe. They were going to paddle right into the guns of the Iroquois. They had to be stopped and brought into the Verchères seigneury. There was no one to go out and stop them.

Madeleine would go herself. She ordered the servant to stand guard at the gate and keep it open.

"If I am killed", she said, "you are to close the gate and go on firing the guns. You must not give up".

She ran to the shore. She was still wearing the helmet and carrying her gun. She stopped the seigneur and his family just in time. She led them into the Verchères fort.

Now she had more people to man the guns. She found guns for them and told them to keep firing. She told them to keep shouting too.

WATCH AT NIGHT

Night was coming. Madeleine knew the Indians were more dangerous at night. They would sneak up close to the fort and try to get through the weak places.

All night Madeleine and her little brothers and the old man kept watch. A strong wind blew and they were very cold.

The guns kept firing. The people in the fort kept shouting. It sounded like a great many people. In this way they fooled the Indians for a while. The neighbour was able to slip out with his family. They went on home.

"YOU ARE WELCOME"

Soon the raids started up again. For eight days and nights the people in the fort kept out the Iroquois. They were a strange little band of fighters.

Early on the morning of the ninth day Madeleine fell asleep. Her gun was across her arms.

Suddenly a signal came from the lookout. Someone was coming to the fort from the river.

"Who is there?" Madeleine called.

The answer made her very happy. At last help had come. Forty soldiers had been sent from Montreal. They had fresh supplies of guns. The Indians drew back. The gate was opened. Madeleine walked down to the river. She met the commander. She gave him her gun.

"Sir, you are welcome. I hand my command over to you."

On Verchères Point, near where the fort stood, is a statue. It is the statue of Madeleine, the fair-haired girl who saved her family's seigneury from the Iroquois.

Montreal's First Nurse

by
Bernice Cleator

E MANCE 1642
NDATRICE

HOSPITALIERE DE SAINT JOSEPH XVIIme S.
HOTEL DIEU DE MONTRÉAL

JEANNE MANCE

Our story begins in a quiet little town in France named Langres.

The most important family in Langres was the Mance family. They held all the important offices in the town. The one who would become the most famous of all was a quiet little girl named Jeanne.

Jeanne Mance was born in 1606. She was the tenth child in a family of thirteen. When she was still a very little girl she wanted to help people. By the time she was fifteen she would help anyone who was sick or hurt. She would take food to needy people.

There were two things she wanted to do. She wanted to become a nurse. She wanted to give her life to God. She had a fine way with people. Everyone loved her.

Before she was thirty she had a chance to show what a good nurse she was. An awful plague came to the town, and to all of France. Hundreds of people died. Jeanne went from house to house nursing the sick. She did not catch the plague. Now she was sure that God wanted her to work for Him.

THE NEW COUNTRY

Soon after this she went to a city some miles from her town. Everyone there was talking of the new country across the sea. They were also talking about Champlain. He had set up a colony in Quebec in 1608. People had gone out from France to help him. Some nurses had gone too.

Now Jeanne knew that she had to go to that new country. There she would care for the sick. She would build a hospital. She would help to build the new colony. She would do God's work in Quebec.

THE COMPANY OF MONTREAL

She went to Paris to visit her cousins.

There she learned of the Company of Montreal. This was a group of rich people in Paris.

One of the people in the Company of Montreal was a very rich lady. Her name was Madame de Bullion. She liked Jeanne at once and wanted to help her with her plans.

The Company wanted to start a colony on the Island of Montreal. They began to make plans. They needed food, medicines, workmen, colonists, and soldiers.

Jeanne Mance was put in charge of the care of the people in the new colony. A man named de Maisonneuve was to be the Governor. The King of France put his seal on all the plans for the new colony of Montreal.

TO NEW FRANCE

Three ships sailed out from France in June, 1641. In one ship were the workmen, the soldiers, the guns and supplies. In the second ship were de Maisonneuve and 25 men. In the third were Jeanne Mance, twelve men and a priest.

The quiet wind in the bay filled the white sails and the ships moved off slowly. Everyone watched from the shore.

Then the ships sailed out of the bay into the huge waves. The ships were thrown around like toys. Jeanne went to her little cabin. She did not come up again for six weeks. She was very sick.

QUEBEC

This is part of Quebec which Jeanne Mance saw from the ship.

In August Jeanne came out on deck. She was very weak and white. The ship was now in the quiet waters of the St. Lawerence River. Here was her new world. She was not at Montreal yet, but she was at Quebec. From the deck she could see Canada's first church standing on a hill. She could see its cross shining in the sun. When the ship landed she climbed the hill to give thanks in the church.

It was too late to go to the Island of Montreal that fall. She and the others had to stay all winter in the little colony at Quebec.

MONTREAL

In May, 1642, they started out for Montreal. There were big flat river boats for supplies. There were long canoes for the people. Each night they camped along the river. They were ten days going from Quebec to Montreal.

Then they could see Montreal's mountain in the middle of the island. After they landed they lost no time getting down to work. Everyone helped. Trees were cut down to make a fence around the camp. Tents were made by the workmen from the bark of the trees. A table was built in the middle of the camp. Jeanne Mance found flowers from the woods to put on it. The next morning the people came to the table to give thanks to God. The priest said Mass. That was the first Mass in Montreal.

More buildings went up. The colony was a happy place. The colonists helped each other with all the work to be done.

IROQUOIS RAIDS

All would have been fine if it had not been for the Iroquois Indians. There were thousands of them. They wanted to drive the white people away. They made raids on the little colony night after night. They killed many people.

The colonists built a better camp. They built a strong stone fort big enough for 100 people. In it they put their food and supplies. Around the fort they built a high fence of trees. Between the fort and the fence were the houses and tents. One house was for de Maisonneuve. Another was for Jeanne Mance. Outside the fence were the farm fields. No one could go out to work in the fields. The Iroquois would kill anyone who did. There were more and more Indian raids. People were hurt or killed every night. Jeanne Mance nursed the sick and the hurt.

HOTEL-DIEU

She sent letters to the Company of Montreal in France. She sent letters to Madame de Bullion. She told of the Indian raids. She told of the need for a hospital in the colony.

Money came and the hospital was built. It had a kitchen, a room for Jeanne Mance, a room for her helpers, and two large rooms for the sick. The Company of Montreal sent out supplies for the new hospital, bedding, medicines, and things for the kitchen. The hospital was named Hotel-Dieu.

Stained glass window in Hotel Dieu in honour of Jeanne Mance.

HELP FROM FRANCE

In 1651 the Iroquois planned to finish off the little colony. 200 Indians made the raid. Jeanne Mance took her sick people into the fort. The colonists fought the Indians bravely. More people were killed. Now the colonists had to move into the fort. They could not stay in the houses or in the fields.

At last de Maisonneuve went back to France to get help for the colony. It was a year before he was back. He had 108 soldiers with him. He also had more workmen and more colonists.

Now they began to build a bigger and better hospital. By 1654 it was ready and Jeanne Mance moved in. But she needed more nurses.

Jeanne Mance made the long trip back to France to see what could be done. Madame de Bullion was very worried when she saw Jeanne. Her work in Montreal had been very hard on her and her health was poor.

Three nursing Sisters were found who would go out to Montreal. Madame de Bullion paid their way.

PLAGUE ON THE HIGH SEAS

On the ship there were Jeanne Mance, her nursing Sisters and 150 other people. A plague broke out on the ship. Almost everyone fell sick. Many died. Part of the ship became a hospital. Jeanne and her nursing Sisters worked night and day. They did not catch the plague.

The ship also had to fight high winds and waves. It was nine weeks before they arrived in Quebec. The ship's captain went back to France. He told of the fine work of Jeanne Mance and her nursing sisters. More help came.

The Mainsonneuve Statue in Montreal

In the fall of 1659 Montreal had almost 300 people. There were 40 houses outside the walls and others inside. There was also a mill. Teachers had come from France and a school had been built. There was a church. There was Jeanne Mance's hospital.

At last a company of soldiers was sent out from France. They began to build forts around Montreal to stop the Indian raids.

Government officers came from Quebec to see the work the nurses were doing. They sent word to the King of France. Jeanne Mance had wanted to start an Order of Nursing Sisters in Montreal. It would be like the Orders of Nursing Sisters in France. She got her wish in a letter with the King's seal on it.

Then three more nursing Sisters came out from France. Two young girls from the colony joined the Order to learn to be nursing Sisters.

Jeanne Mance was in charge of the hospital until the day she died. She died in 1673.

The Hotel-Dieu Hospital still stands in Montreal. It still cares for people both rich and poor. In its garden is a monument to Jeanne Mance.

Two Brave Heroes
Montcalm

by
Freda Hudson

EARLY DAYS IN FRANCE

Two men who changed the history of Canada were born over three thousand miles away. Their armies met in Quebec in the war between the French and English.

On the 26th of February, in the year 1712, a boy was born in a castle. The castle was in France near a city called Nimes. The boy's father was named Louis Daniel. His mother was called Marie Therese. He was baptized Louis Joseph. The family name was Montcalm. Most Canadians call Louis, Montcalm.

The young Montcalm was not a healthy child. He was taken to live with his grandmother in the country. She treated him like a sickly child and spoiled him. He was a clever boy, but he could not read or write at the age of six. In those days, the children of the rich were taught at a very early age to read and write. They had lessons in the home, with private teachers. His grandmother did not have a teacher for him.

His father was upset to learn that his son was not being taught. He hired a teacher for Montcalm. He never learned how to write capital letters. He would begin a sentence with a small letter. He would use a small letter to write his name. He soon learned how to read his own language. He also learned to read Greek and Latin.

At the age of fifteen he joined the army. He was a junior officer. While he was in the army he continued to study. He learned to read and speak German.

FAMILY

When his father died he returned to the castle near Nimes. It now belonged to him. He lived there for a few years with his young wife. She was called Angelique. They had ten children. Four of them died very young. The children who lived were two boys and four girls. He was a very kind father and he thought often of the future of his family.

He joined his Regiment again and fought in Europe. He was wounded several times.

In 1748 he was once again living with his wife and children at his home.

In 1756 he received a letter from the King of France. The letter told him that he had been chosen to command the troops in North America. He was given the rank of Major-General.

His wife was very sad that he would be so far away from her and the children. His mother thought that this was a great honour for her son. She was sad to see him go, but she wanted him to take the post. He took the advice of his mother. His wife never forgave her mother-in-law for advising him that way.

AT WAR WITH THE ENGLISH

Six sailing ships crossed the Atlantic with Montcalm and his men. Montcalm's ship was named the Licorne. He landed in Canada on May 13, 1756.

The city of Quebec in 1756 was small. There was a wall around it. Inside the walls there were many soldiers and Indians. They were getting ready to fight the English.

Fighting between the French and the English

had been going on for a long time. The struggle for North America lasted for nearly seventy-five years. It was called the French and Indian Wars.

This period was very bad for the early settlers. It was not easy for them to plant their crops. It was not easy for them to care for their farms. The French and English soldiers were fighting. There were raids by the Indians. Some Indian tribes fought with the French. Some tribes fought with the English.

Ten days after Montcalm arrived in Quebec City he went to Montreal to meet the Governor of Canada. The King of France had written a letter to the Governor. He told him that Montcalm must take his orders from him. Montcalm went to meet with him so that they could plan their campaign against the English.

Quebec City as Montcalm first saw it.

VICTORIES

Montcalm was one of the greatest commanders of his time. He proved this soon after his arrival in Canada. In August 1756 he captured the Fort at Oswega, New York from the English.

The next year he captured Fort William Henry on Lake George, New York. At that battle, the Indians who were fighting on his side killed the English prisoners. This act was against Montcalm's orders. He did not want the prisoners killed. It upset him very much. At the risk of his own life he was able to bring the Indians under control.

One of the forts that the English attacked was Fort Carillon at Ticonderoga. There were about thrity-five hundred men in the English army. On July 8, 1758 the English attacked. The battle began at noon. All day the lines of English soldiers marched towards the fort. As they got closer to the walls the French fired at them. The front ranks fell. The heat was terrible. At one point Montcalm took off his jacket and said to his soldiers with a smile "We will have a warm time of it today, my friends."

The fight lasted for three days. The English lost one thousand, nine hundred and forty-four men. The French lost one hundred and four killed and two hundred and forty-eight wounded. This was a great victory for the French. With small supplies from France, the French could not hold out against the large numbers of the English.

The French needed more supplies from France. Montcalm wrote to the King that the people were short of food. The soldiers had no shoes. In reply to this France sent a small supply of food and seventy-five men. The English had sent many men and a lot of money to be used in these wars.

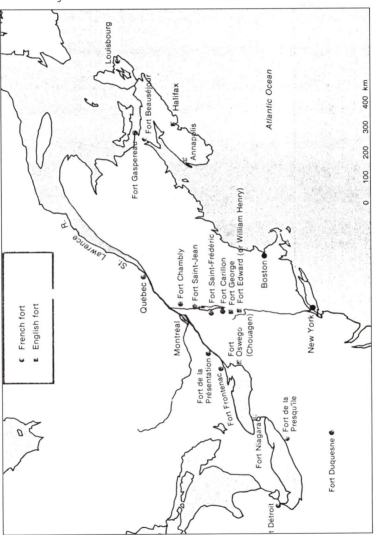

This map shows Montcalm's victories over the English.

A BRAVE HERO

The government of England ordered that Quebec City be attacked. This would not be easy. The city was high on a rocky cliff. It was almost impossible to climb the cliff. Many English ships were sailing towards Canada. Montcalm's army was split up. They were trying to defend many towns. As the English got closer, most of the families in the city of Quebec fled to the country. The streets were blocked with carts trying to take furniture out of the houses. The nursing nuns left their convents and moved into the General Hospital.

General Wolfe, in charge of the English, ordered his troops to land at the beach at the foot of the cliff. It was at night. There was no moon. Twenty-four volunteers climbed the cliffs. They had their guns strapped to their backs. They grabbed hold of branches and shrubs to help themselves up the cliff. Then about sixteen hundred men followed them.

When Montcalm was told that the English had climbed the steep cliffs, he did not believe it. More and more messengers brought news of the English. When Montcalm went out to meet them he was surprised to see that General Wolfe's whole army was there. The French did not have as many soldiers. Some of them did not have bayonets. Montcalm rode his horse in front of the French lines. He held his sword in the air and waved his men on.

At 10 o'clock that morning, the two armies faced each other. Before the battle was over, the English General was killed. Montcalm was wounded. He was taken to the home of a doctor. He asked that letters be written to his mother and to his wife and family.

He died at 5 o'clock in the morning on September 14, 1759. He was 47 years old. His name is remembered in history as a brave hero.

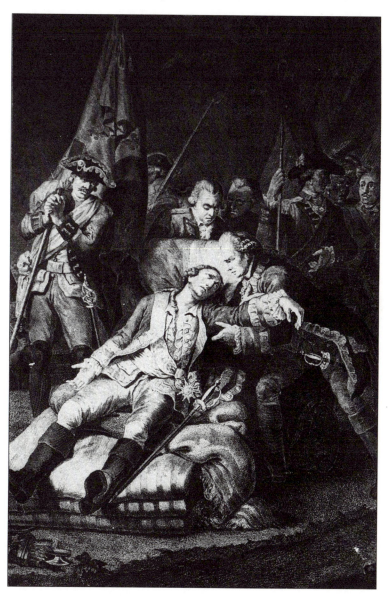

Montcalm is wounded.

Two Brave Heroes
Wolfe

by
Freda Hudson

J.Chapman sculp!

EARLY DAYS

The English General who died in Quebec was James Wolfe. He was born on January 2, 1727. His mother was named Henrietta Thompson. His father was Edward Wolfe. Edward was an officer in the Marines. The boy wanted to be like his father. He joined the army when he was fifteen. (When he was twenty-three years old he was an officer.)

He was not very strong, but he was brave. He was a good soldier. He was tall and very thin. His hair was red. His skin was very pale. He was friendly and easy to get along with. He made many friends. He worked hard. He studied Latin and French and mathematics.

In the winter of 1753 he lived in Paris. He met the King of France. He took riding lessons and learned to dance. When he returned to England his army went to Scotland to fight the Scots. He was making a name for himself as a leader. He was kind to his men and not cruel to the enemy.

Statue of Wolfe in his birthplace, Sevenoakes, England.

LOUISBOURG IS TAKEN

War between France and England began. The Prime Minister of England asked Wolfe to sail to Canada. The English wanted to own Canada. Wolfe was not happy to go across the sea. He was seasick. His job was to take the Fort at Louisbourg from the French. Louisbourg was at the beginning of the Gulf of St. Lawrence. In 1758 Louisbourg was won by the English.

RETURN TO ENGLAND

Wolfe returned to England. He went to the city of Bath to rest. He was tired from the long sea trip. When he was in Bath he asked Catherine Lowther to marry him. She said yes. She gave him her picture. He carried it with him until he died. He liked children. He wanted to have a home of his own.

FIRST DUTY TO COUNTRY

His duty to his country came first. He was ready to do what his country wanted. The Prime Minister asked him to go again to Canada. Even though he was not well he got ready to go. His mother and father were afraid that they would never see him again. He felt the same way.

On February 17, 1759, the ship "Neptune" sailed from England. Wolfe was standing on the deck. He tried to forget his sea-sickness. There were twenty-two battleships, five frigates and nineteen other ships. Wolfe was in charge of all of them.

Wolfe landed at Louisbourg in May. The first news he heard was that his father had died. He was very sad. He was sorry he had not been with his

The English Fleet at Quebec.

father. He felt badly that he could not help his mother.

The English fleet sailed up the St. Lawrence River. In June the English fleet landed at the Island of Orleans. Wolfe could see the city of Quebec from the island. He sent a message to the French-Canadians. The message said that England was at war with France. He said that England was not at war with them, the people. He told them how many English soldiers there were in North America. He said that England would not harm the people of Canada. He told them that their religion would not be changed. The women and children would not be hurt. The people could stay on their land and in their houses. He said that France could not help them. What he said was true, but the Canadians did not want to give in.

THE PLAINS OF ABRAHAM

Outside the walls of Quebec City there was a level piece of land. This field had been owned by one of the early settlers. His name was Abraham Martin. He had cleared the land. It was almost three quarters of a mile wide. On the right side was a steep cliff. This cliff dropped down to the St. Lawrence River. It was on this piece of land that Wolfe and Montcalm would fight. It was that steep cliff that Wolfe and his men would climb. In the history books this fight would be known as the Battle of the Plains of Abraham.

There had been French soldiers posted on the Plain. But they had been moved away. If they had been kept there Wolfe would have lost the war. His men would have been killed as they climbed the cliff. There was no one to stop them. Soon his soldiers were everywhere.

WOLFE'S DEATH

Wolfe marched at the head of his soldiers. In his bright red coat he was easy to see. He was so tall. Two of his officers were wounded. Wolfe was hit on the wrist. He bandaged it with his handkerchief. A second bullet hit him. He did not stop. A third bullet hit him in the chest. He did not want his men to see him fall. He asked one of his officers to help him. Three of his men helped him. They laid him on the grass. He was told that the French were running away. He told one of his men to run and give orders to cut off the retreat. He turned on his side. He said "God be praised. I die happy."

He was thirty-two years old.

England was sad to hear of Wolfe's death. His mother and his bride-to-be were very unhappy. His mother had lost a good son.

Death of Wolfe.

TWO CANADIAN HEROES

Wolfe became a hero in England. Montcalm became a hero in Quebec, even though the war had been lost.

Wolfe and Montcalm were great men. They were both sickly children. They did not let anything stop them from doing what they believed in. They will always be remembered as Canadian heroes.

Today there is a statue with the names of both generals. In part, the words on the statue says "Courage gave them a common death, a common fame..."

Monument to Wolfe and Montcalm on the Plains of Abraham.

Thomas Peters
A Black Loyalist

by
Gladys E. Neale

Halifax as Thomas Peters probably saw it.

NOTE: Unfortunately it was not possible to find a photograph of Thomas Peters nor photographs of the incidents in this story.

FIGHTING FOR THE BRITISH

This is the story of a black soldier and leader. Thomas Peters was born in 1738 in West Africa. His father was the chief of a tribe. When a young man Thomas was kidnapped. He was sold as a slave in America.

In 1776 war between the British and American colonists began. Thomas was 38 years old. At that time he was told that the British would free any slave owned by the rebels. This brought joy to Peters' heart. He began to plan his escape. He ran away from his master.

Soon Thomas reached New York. There he joined the Black Pioneers. He fought for the British for seven years. During that time he was made a sergeant and married. His wife was also in the Black Pioneers.

When the war ended, the British promised to take the Black Pioneers to one of their colonies. The ship carrying Peters and his wife to safety went first to Bermuda. Then they were taken to Annapolis Royal in Nova Scotia. There were 3500 Black Pioneers who were brought to Nova Scotia after the war.

THE STRUGGLE FOR LAND

Thomas Peters was placed in charge of some of these settlers. With 200 Black Pioneers, he came to live near Digby, Nova Scotia.

From the beginning the black Loyalists were not treated the same as the white Loyalists. Loyalists were given three years of food and other goods. This was to keep them while they were building their homes and farms. The blacks were given only enough to last for 80 days. They also had to earn their living by working on the roads. At the same time they were trying to work on their own land.

Peters went to the Governor of Nova Scotia to ask for land grants. One acre plots were given to 76 black families. This was not enough land for farming. So they grew vegetables on their small plots. They also fished in the Bay of Fundy. They formed churches and built a school.

Peters tried many times to get land in Nova Scotia for the black Loyalists. Then he went to New Brunswick. Again he could not get enough land. Only one third of the black Loyalists received any land at all.

TO LONDON FOR JUSTICE

Peters waited for six years and made five requests to the governors. Then he decided to go to the British government. He sailed to London where he presented his request. He spoke for several hundred black people.

In England Thomas Peters was given good news. There were plans to set up a colony of freed slaves on the west coast of Africa. The British government would pay the costs of getting the black Loyalists to Sierra Leone.

In 1791 Peters returned to Annapolis and Saint John to tell his friends about this plan. The black Loyalists were eager to accept this offer of free land. They were told they would have full British rights in Sierra Leone. 1200 of them gathered in Halifax, Nova Scotia. In January, 1792, they set out in 15 ships for Sierra Leone.

SIERRA LEONE

Here, too, promises made to the new colonists were not kept. Thomas Peters, as their leader, went to the white people in charge of the colony. He asked them to give to his people the land and rights promised to them. These had brought them to this country. Again he was turned down.

The white people then tried to turn his own black friends against him. Peters was accused of stealing from the trunk of a settler. This man had died of fever. Peters said he had loaned some things to his friend. He was only taking back what were his. He was not believed. The white people made him return the goods. What upset Peters more was that he was rebuked in public. This was a blow to his pride.

Soon after he became ill with fever and died. Sadly he had lost the respect of the people he had led to Africa. They believed the white people rather than the man who had tried to do so much for them.

THE COLONY FAILS

Other disasters made life hard for the colonists. There was lack of rain, tornadoes and fever. Many of them died, as Thomas Peters had.

The colony failed in its first year. Even so there are still people in Sierra Leone whose forefathers came from Nova Scotia. Thomas Peters left his mark on the history of Canada and Africa. He was a slave, a soldier, a Loyalist and a leader.

The Story of Laura Secord

by
Bernice Cleator

LAURA SECORD.

THE WAR OF 1812

In 1812 Canada was at war with the United States. The war was mostly between the Americans and the British. Canada belonged to the British. There wasn't much of Canada then. There were only a few settlements along the border.

One of those settlements was the village of Queenston. Queenston is on the bank of the Niagara River. It is at the foot of a very high hill.

James and Laura Secord lived in Queenston. They lived in a house just under that hill. James and Laura had five children. James had a little business selling flour and other goods in the village.

In 1812, James was away at war. Laura did not know where he was.

The Secord House at Queenston.

THE BATTLE AT QUEENSTON

The thirteenth of October, 1812, was a day the village of Queenston would never forget. On that day the war came to the village.

Early in the morning hundreds of American soldiers came across the river in boats. They landed at Queenston. At once the noise, the shouting and the shooting began. The British and the Canadians came on foot and on horseback to fight the Americans.

Laura Secord woke up to the sound of guns. She could hear the horses' feet and the shouts of the men.

Now she had to think of her children. She ran to their bedrooms and woke them up. The oldest was thirteen, the youngest only two. Laura and her five children went out the back door into a little road behind the village. They ran to a farm about a mile away. Guns went off all around them. They waited at the farm for most of the day.

Laura was a slim young woman of 37, with thick brown hair. She was worried about James in the middle of the fighting.

LAURA LOOKS FOR JAMES

At last the guns were quiet. Laura could wait no longer. She left the children at the farm and ran all the way to the village.

The Americans had been driven back, but soldiers from both sides lay dead all over the fields. Many others were crying out in pain.

She looked and looked until she found her

James. He lay there, badly hurt and very weak. Another soldier helped her to get James to their house.

Laura got James into bed and did what she could for him. She was a good nurse but she had very little to work with. Laura cared for James all winter. At last he was better but still very weak.

By the spring of 1813 the war had moved on about twenty miles west to a place called Beaver Dams.

Sitting room in Secord home.

WHAT WAS WAR LIKE IN THOSE DAYS?

Soldiers moved on foot or on horse-back. They carried long guns and bayonets. The big field guns were on wheels. They were pulled by four or six horses. The soldiers fought hand-to-hand, shooting guns or using bayonets. They shot horses out from under the men. They broke into houses to get what they needed. They burned fences and bridges. They made deep holes in the dirt roads with their big wheels.

The men and boys were all away fighting. Who was looking after the farms? The women were doing the best they could.

At Beaver Dams, there was a British officer named FitzGibbon. He had put fifty men in a big house on a hill. In the house were stores of guns and food. The men were to watch the American soldiers and make as much trouble for them as they could.

IMPORTANT INFORMATION

Back in Queenston Laura Secord found out something important. Some American officers came to her house wanting something to eat. She set everything she had on the big kitchen table for them. Then she stood just outside the window while they ate. The American general was giving orders to his officers. They were to take 500 men and attack FitzGibbon. FitzGibbon had only fifty men on the hill. It looked so easy, and they laughed as they ate.

But they didn't know Laura Secord. When the Americans had gone she ran to James.

"Someone has to get to FitzGibbon and tell him the Americans are coming to attack him."

"I WILL GO"

James could not go. He was still weak. He could not use one arm and one leg.

"I will go", said Laura.

She would go first thing in the morning. She would say she was going to see her brother in the next village if the Americans stopped her.

By 4:30 in the morning the sun was up. It was the month of June. Laura had on a house-dress she had made herself. It was brown with little orange flowers. It was long, almost to the ground. On her head was a white sun bonnet. On her feet were thin slippers.

Laura walked to her brother's house. She hoped he would go and tell FitzGibbon. But her brother was sick in bed. Laura would have to go on.

She walked through woods and wet places. She walked on dirt roads. She was afraid to use better roads. The day was hot as the sun rose higher in the sky. She had to stop and rest. Her slippers came off in the mud. She was afraid of the animals in the woods. She was afraid of meeting Indians. She had hills to climb and a small river to cross.

She walked all day. By the time she crossed the little river it was dark. She had walked almost twenty miles.

HELP FROM THE INDIANS

She walked right into an Indian camp in the dark. She was sure that would be the end of her.

"I cannot give up now", she said to herself. She went up to the chief. She tried to tell him what she had to do. She could not speak his language. At last he understood. FitzGibbon, his men and the Indians would all be killed if 500 Americans attacked them. The chief went with her to FitzGibbon at Beaver Dams.

FitzGibbon could not believe his eyes. Here was a woman he had never seen. Her dress was dirty and torn. She had nothing on her feet. She was very tired.

FitzGibbon listened to her story. He had some of his men take her to a farm not far away for the night. Then he and the Indian chief decided what to do. He had only fifty men. But there were 400 Indians. FitzGibbon, and his men and the Indians would all work together.

By the next morning they were all in place. The Indians were not in line like soldiers. They were hidden in the woods all along both sides of the dirt road.

DEFEAT OF THE AMERICANS

Soon they saw the Americans. The first ones were on horseback. Then came 300 foot soldiers. Following the men were the big field guns on wheels. They were pulled by horses. At the end came more men on horseback. They had only two more miles to go. Then they would surprise FitzGibbon.

It was the Americans who were surprised. From the woods the shots came on all sides. They came from the front and from the back. The Americans fought bravely but they couldn't keep up with the Indians. Many men were killed and many were hurt. At last they gave up. The battle was over. The Americans had lost. They were driven back across the Niagara River. Then the war moved off to the east.

Queenston, Beaver Dams and Niagara were all quiet again. Laura Secord's long walk had saved them.

LAURA BECOMES FAMOUS

What became of Laura Secord?

She went back home to her family in Queenston. They lived on quietly until James died.

It was not until many years later that the story of Laura Secord's walk became known. Men writing the history of the War of 1812 told of Laura's walk. The Prince of Wales came to see her. When he went back home he sent a fine gift of gold money. More and more people read of what she had done. Her fame grew.

Laura Secord died at the age of 93.

Years later the Government of Canada put up a fine monument to her memory. The monument stands high on the hill above Queenston. On the monument is a picture of Laura Secord, wearing the clothes she wore on her walk.

Laura Secord Monument on Queenston heights.

Nellie McClung

by
Gladys E. Neale

CHILDHOOD

Nellie Mooney was born on October 20, 1873. Her father and mother lived on a farm near Owen Sound, Ontario. There were six children in the Mooney family when Nellie came along. She was the baby of the family.

Even though the youngest, Nellie still had to do her share of the family chores. Her mother always kept the children busy. One of Nellie's jobs was to water the ashes from which her mother made soap. The Mooneys made everything they could because they did not have much money.

In the East people began to hear how rich the soil was in the West. First Will, the oldest boy, went West to Manitoba. The rest of the family followed in 1880. On their new farm Nellie had a happy time. One of her jobs was to bring the cows to the barn. Then she helped to milk them. In harvest time, she took lunch to the men in the fields.

SCHOOL DAYS

The great event in their first few years in Manitoba was the building of a school. Nellie was ten years old when she first went to school.

Because there were no fences, Nellie kept the cows from going into the fields. She could not go to school for some months during the year. How sad she was to see the other children going to school. She kept up her studies as well as she could. Her sister Hannah helped her with her arithmetic.

Very early she wanted to write stories. Soon she began to write poetry.

The other girls at school were doing fancy work

Nellie came to this country store to pick up the mail.

at noon. They did beautiful lace and table mats. Nellie wanted to do pretty work too. She found that she couldn't do handwork. The other girls teased her. Nellie knew what she was good at, spelling, reading, writing and arithmetic. She was soon at the top of her class.

One Friday afternoon she recited her own poem:

"The heights by great men reached and kept
Were not attained by sudden flight,
But they, while their companions slept,
Were toiling upward in the night
They did not leave their reading books
To fool around with crochet hooks;
They did not slight their history-notes
To make lace for their petticoats;
But step by step they did advance
And gave no thought to coat or pants:
So let my steps be ever led
Away from wool, and crochet thread;
And let my heart be set to find
The higher treasures of the mind."

70

SCHOOL TEACHER

With her sisters' help, Nellie was able to go to Winnipeg. There she learned to be a teacher. Before her seventeenth birthday, she was in charge of a one-room school. She taught eight grades.

Later she went to Manitou to teach. The McClung family lived there. Nellie arranged to board with them. Wes, their oldest son, worked in the drugstore. From the first time she met him, Nellie liked Wes. The McClung's place became her second home. Mr. and Mrs. McClung were like parents to her.

Nellie's friendship with Wes grew. Their marriage took place on August 25, 1896. One of her friends was sorry to hear about this event. She thought Nellie should become a writer. In those days, marriage ended any thought of a woman having another career. Nellie Mooney McClung showed them!!!

WIFE AND MOTHER

There was never any thought that Nellie would continue to teach. School boards would not keep a married woman on the staff. Nellie didn't fight this. Now she would have time to study and to write. This was not to be!

In June of 1897, their first child, Jack, was born. Her days were busy caring for the baby and doing her other household tasks. There was little time for her reading and writing.

By 1911, Nellie and Wes had five children, four boys and one girl. There were not too many rules in the home but when one was made, it had to be kept. It was a happy family.

CRUSADER

Nellie McClung began her crusading life by joining the WCTU, Women's Christian Temperance Union. Some men thought the initials stood for "Women Continually Torment Us."

Women came together to make life easier, safer and better for boys and girls. The first speech Nellie made was at a WCTU convention. She bought a smart new dress and hat because she wanted to be easy on the eye. That was her style throughout her public life.

This 1913 cartoon shows Nellie's crusade for temperance.

AUTHOR

It was her mother-in-law who encouraged Nellie to write a short story for a contest. It did not win a prize but became the first chapter in her first book "Sowing Seeds in Danny". It was published in 1908 by a Canadian publisher. It was an immediate success.

Because of this, Nellie received many requests to give public readings from "Sowing Seeds in Danny". One comment on her speeches was "It isn't what she says so much as the way she says it. She has a wonderful personality." Her books and her lecture tours made her well-known throughout the West. Nellie was becoming famous.

WOMEN'S RIGHTS

Wes McClung changed his job. The family moved to Winnipeg. Nellie soon became a part of the women's movement there. There were many laws which did not treat women well. One was that they could not vote. All over the world women were fighting for this right. In many countries they had won the fight.

Early in 1914 Nellie and several hundred women asked the Manitoba Government to give women the right to vote. The Premier dismissed them saying, "Now you forget all this nonsense about women voting. Nice women don't want to vote."

The women were angry. They decided humour might be a better way to get the government to change its mind. They rented a theatre in Winnipeg. There they staged a mock parliament. All members were women. Nellie was the Premier.

Now it was the men who were asking for the right to vote. Nellie used the same reasons the Premier had — "Politics unsettle men, and this will mean unpaid bills, broken furniture, broken vows and divorce. Men's place is on the farm."

The play was a great success. The audience laughed and laughed. The Premier and his government were put in a poor light. Nellie and her cast were asked to bring the play to many parts of the province.

The women, with Nellie as their leader, fought on. Soon they were given the right to vote in Manitoba, in Alberta, and in Canada.

These three, Nellie McClung, Irene Pailby and Emily Murphy worked to win women the right to vote in Canada.

Nellie with a group of family members and supporters in front of the McClung's home in Edmonton.

NELLIE IN POLITICS

Once more the McClung family moved. This time Wes was sent to Edmonton. Soon Nellie was working in Alberta for temperance, and for women's right to vote. In 1921 she ran as a Liberal in one of the ridings in Edmonton. She won but the Liberals were defeated. She was a good member of the provincial government.

In the election of 1926, Nellie was defeated. One lesson she learned from either joy or sorrow was to go on. Her club work kept her as busy as ever. She led a large Bible class in her church. She now gave more time to her writing.

LANTERN LANE

Then Wes was transferred to Victoria, B.C. Her doctor advised Nellie to slow down. Even so she continued writing. She went on speaking tours. In the 1935 federal election campaign, she helped the Liberal party.

In 1935 Wes and Nellie bought Lantern Lane, a small farm outside Victoria. There they found peace and contentment.

Nellie wrote her own story in two books. These were widely read.

Just before she died, she said to Wes "Oh, I'm still here! I'll never believe I'm dead till I see it in the paper." She died in September, 1951.

On her tombstone in Victoria are the simple words "Loved and Remembered".

Nellie and Wes in front of Lantern Lane.

Family Reunion at Lantern Lane.

The Story of Madame Vanier

by
Bernice Cleator

A SUPPORTER

Some people are born to be leaders. Some are followers. Some are supporters.

Supporters need to be strong. They must stand with their leader through thick and thin.

Madame Georges Vanier is a supporter.

She was born in Montreal in 1898. Her name was Pauline Archer. She was the only daughter of Judge Archer and his wife.

Pauline grew up in a fine big house in Montreal. She went to a Convent school for four years. Then she was taught by a governess in her own home.

Christmas was always a happy time. All the Archers would go to their grandfather's big home in Quebec City. Pauline and her ten cousins had a great time together.

Before they went, Judge Archer made sure that all the poor children of the parish church had a Christmas gift from his big Christmas tree.

When Pauline was a very young girl, she dreamed of helping people. Maybe she would be a nun. Maybe she would go across the world to help people far away.

She grew up to be very tall and straight, with a strong beautiful face. She was the kind of girl everyone admired.

Pauline was 22 when she met Major Georges Vanier. Georges was in command of one company of the Royal 22nd Regiment. This regiment was called the Van Doos. Georges was tall too, and very handsome in his uniform. He was already a war hero. He had lost a leg in World War I, and had been decorated by King George V.

EARLY LIFE AT GOVERNMENT HOUSE

In September, 1921 Georges and Pauline were married.

For a year they lived in Ottawa. Georges was on the staff of the Governor General, Lord Byng. They became very close friends of Lord and Lady Byng. Each morning early, Lord Byng would ride past their little cottage in the grounds of Government House. He would toss a pebble at their window and call out, "Get up, you little Vaniers".

Georges and Pauline were both French and English. Georges' mother was English and his father was French. Pauline's mother was French and her father was English. They spoke, read and wrote in both French and English. Georges was a great help to Lord Byng who did not speak French.

ENGLAND FOR THE FIRST TIME

Their time with the Governor General came to an end. Georges was to join the staff of a military college in England.

In 1923 Pauline and Georges were off to England. They lived in a house on the grounds of the college. Their daughter Thérèse was born there. Lord Byng wrote that the accents on her name were like his cat's eyebrows!

QUEBEC CITY

By 1925 the Vaniers were back in Quebec City. Georges, now a Lieutenant-Colonel, was put in command of the Van Doos. Later that year their first son was born. His godparents were Lord and Lady Byng, so he became known as Byngsie. His real name was Georges, like his father's. A second son, Bernard, was born in Quebec City in 1927.

SWITZERLAND

Now it was time to say good-bye to the military life in Quebec City. A new life was to begin in Switzerland. Georges Vanier was to represent Canada at the League of Nations. The hope was that the League of Nations would put an end to war.

In 1928 the Vaniers set off by ship, with three children and two nurses.

A third son, Jean, was born in Switzerland. Lord Byng wrote to Pauline: "My dear, I think you are starting a little League of Nations of your own".

ENGLAND AGAIN

Back in Canada the Prime Minister had plans for the Vaniers. They would go next to London, England. Georges would represent Canada in London. Pauline would take her place beside him.

In 1932 the family moved to London. They had a house with a garden and many trees. The three older children were all in London schools. Life was happy and busy. Thérèse wrote little plays for her brothers to put on. At bed-time Pauline and Georges read stories to the children.

PARIS, 1939

In January 1939 the Vaniers moved to Paris. They were to represent Canada in France. They were the right people for the job. A Canadian newspaper said, "Paris will give the best of welcomes to our new representative and to Madame Vanier who is the perfect wife of a perfect diplomat".

By August 1939, Georges Vanier was telling all Canadians in Paris to leave at once. World War II was about to begin.

ESCAPE FROM FRANCE

The German army marched into Paris in June 1940. It was time for Pauline and the children to leave. Georges got word that a British ship was coming across to France to take refugees to England. Pauline and the family packed what they could and drove to the harbour. 300 refugees were packed into every space on board. Three bombs dropped on the dock before they got away. More fell around them on the way, but the ship landed safely in England.

As soon as he could, Georges joined Pauline in England. By then the bombs were dropping on London every night. The Vaniers sent their children to Pauline's mother in Montreal.

Pauline began to work for the Red Cross. She visited and helped soldiers who had been hurt. She worked beside her husband. He said, "We work as one". They spent most nights in bomb shelters. They took homeless people into their home.

HOME TO QUEBEC

The Canadian government then called the Vaniers home to Canada. Georges was made Brigadier-General and put in command of the military district of Quebec. From then on he was known as General Vanier.

Pauline, or Madame Vanier, was now 43 years old. Her fifth child was born in August, 1941. He was called Michel. His oldest brother and sister were his godparents.

In her Red Cross uniform Madame Vanier honours Canadians who died at Dieppe.

PARIS, 1946

General Vanier was sent back to Paris as soon as the war was over. Paris was still not safe, and the general planned to go alone. But no! Madame Vanier would go too. She went in the uniform of the Red Cross. She worked for the Paris Red Cross. In Paris, the marks of war were everywhere. Madame Vanier collected clothing and gave it to needy people. She visited the sick and those wounded in the war. Food and clothes came from Canada.

When things settled down the children began coming from Canada. It was three years since the Vaniers had seen their baby, Michel. In the car from the airport, the little boy said to his father, "You and I are going to be friends, aren't we?"

The Paris years ended in 1953 and the Vaniers returned to Montreal. General Vanier was now retired and they were living quietly. But not for long.

THE GOVERNOR GENERAL AND HIS SUPPORTER

In 1959 General Vanier became Governor General of Canada.

They moved back to Ottawa and into Government House. This was where they had begun their married life 38 years before. It was to be their home for eight years.

During those eight years, Pauline Vanier showed what a strong supporter she was. She travelled with her husband all across Canada and into the native settlements of the far north.

She looked after guests from all over the world — Kings and Queens, and heads of governments. They had 7000 guests a year. She opened buildings and named ships. She spoke to groups of all kinds. The Vaniers tried to bring the French and English people together. They wanted them to understand each other.

Madame Vanier on tour in Northern Alberta.

Pauline Vanier still wanted to help people. She worked for the Canadian Cancer Society, the Family Service, and the St. John's Ambulance. In 1966 she was named Woman of the Year.

The Vaniers always tried to gather the family together in the summer. They would live a simple life in a country house on the St. Lawrence River.

Michel, the baby, was now an officer in the Van Doos. Thérèse was a doctor, soon to go to Africa. Bernard was an artist living in France with his wife and children. Jean was a university professor, and Byngsie was a monk near Montreal.

By 1967 the Governor General was getting tired. He worked in his bedroom, and had Mass said there every day. His wife stayed beside him. In March he died.

Now Madame Vanier had to go on alone. Could she still be a supporter?

The Governor General and Madame Vanier meet with the Indian Chiefs.

SUPPORTER IN TROSLY, FRANCE

In 1964 her son Jean had given up his work as a university professor. He went to the small town of Trosly, in the north of France. He opened his home to two young, mentally handicapped men. He called the home L'Arche (The Ark). He hoped it would aid the helpless. This home was the first of 88 L'Arche homes in 21 countries. Each is different from the others.

Trosly, the first L'Arche community, now has 28 homes shared by 400 people. Some L'Arche communities have only a small apartment. This is shared by two or three handicapped people and a few helpers.

They all work the same way. They are all homes where the handicapped can find help in healing their hurts. For many, a L'Arche community is the first home they have ever known. At last they find love and peace.

Many helpers are needed. The helpers come from all walks of life. Some are young, some are older. The oldest helper at Trosly, France, is Madame Pauline Vanier. In 1972 she moved to Trosly. She was 74. It was time to rest after her busy life.

When she got to Trosly she found she was needed. Her love and her strong support were just what her son Jean needed in his L'Arche community. A hug from Madame Vanier could turn a bad day into a good one. It worked for the handicapped, and it worked for the helpers. So she stayed on.

Today she has her own cosy house at Trosly. She is past 90, but still tall and straight. Her hair is shiny white. She offers a motherly ear and a cup of tea to anyone who drops in.

She is still a strong supporter.

Biographies

Bernice Cleator (Mrs. K.J.) is a retired classroom teacher and is now a literacy tutor. She is Secretary of the North Bay and Area Literacy Council.

M.J. Collins (Mike) has been a Laubach volunteer for ten years. He is an ex-farmer, retired civil servant, and a WWII veteran. He has had short stories and articles published in North America.

Freda Hudson emigrated from England at the age of six. She has five children and seven grandchildren. She is past chairperson of the Townshipper Reading Council, and is now a Director of Laubach Literacy of Canada. Freda is also an active tutor.

Gladys Neale has been in educational publishing for most of her career mainly with Macmillan of Canada. There she became a Director and eventually Senior Vice-President. She has been active in the field of literacy since 1972. She is now a Director of Laubach Literacy of Canada.